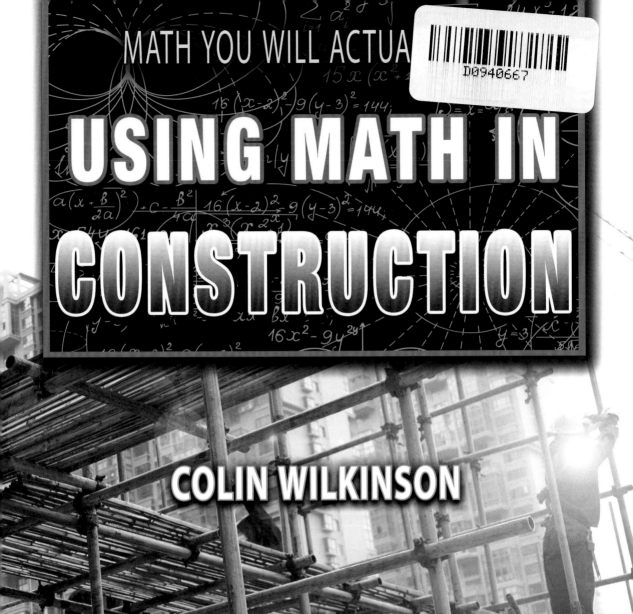

MATH YOU WILL ACTUA

USING MATH IN CONSTRUCTION

COLIN WILKINSON

rosen publishing's

rosen central®

NEW YORK

Published in 2018 by The Rosen Publishing Group, Inc.
29 East 21st Street, New York, NY 10010

Library of Congress Cataloging-in-Publication Data

Names: Wilkinson, Colin, 1977–
Title: Using math in construction / Colin Wilkinson.
Description: New York : Rosen Central, [2018] | Series: Math you will actually use | Audience: Grades 5–8. | Includes bibliographical references and index.
Identifiers: LCCN 2016059975 | ISBN 9781499438529 (pbk. book) | ISBN 9781499438543 (library bound book) | ISBN 9781499438536 (6 pack)
Subjects: LCSH: Building—Mathematics—Juvenile literature. | Engineering mathematics—Juvenile literature.
Classification: LCC TH149 .W55 2018 | DDC 624.01/51—dc23
LC record available at https://lccn.loc.gov/2016059975

Manufactured in the United States of America

METRIC CONVERSION CHART	
1 inch = 2.54 centimeters; 25.4 millimeters	1 cup = 250 milliliters
1 foot = 30.48 centimeters	1 ounce = 28 grams
1 yard = .914 meters	1 fluid ounce = 30 milliliters
1 square foot = .093 square meters	1 teaspoon = 5 milliliters
1 square mile = 2.59 square kilometers	1 tablespoon = 15 milliliters
1 ton = .907 metric tons	1 quart = .946 liters
1 pound = 454 grams	355 degrees Fahrenheit = 180 degrees Celsius
1 mile = 1.609 kilometers	

CONTENTS

INTRODUCTION

The world of construction brings people skyscrapers and massive bridges but also smaller projects such as building a doghouse or designing a playground. Imagine building something as simple as a chair. How long should the legs be so that it is easy to sit down on it without a drastic fall, and stand up from sitting without too much effort? What is the correct amount of material needed for the seat to keep someone from falling through when sitting? How are all of the components fastened together? Applying some basic mathematical concepts when planning and building supplies the answers to these questions.

Suppose your school is planning for a fall festival, and you have volunteered to create a suction-cup archery booth. You've been told you have a space to work in along the edge of the field, and it is 15 feet wide and 30 feet long. What now? You know you'll need posts and tape or ribbon to run around the edges to ensure nobody accidentally wanders across the range. You'll need a table at one end to greet participants. You'll also need to design and paint a board to present fun targets and find a way to stand it upright.

To best plan the booth, and determine which materials and how many you'll need, you have to use math. To determine the length of tape for the perimeter, determine the total length of the

Setting up for archery requires more than just randomly plopping down targets. Determine safe distances from the archer to the target, along with proper spacing between each target, ahead of time with math.

booth's edges. Rely on division and some basic algebra to calculate the number of posts and how to space them evenly along the tape. Before building you may create a design on paper, similar to a map that shows the position of each element. The map would likely have some indication of how big each element is to show where it should be placed within the booth area.

Now imagine skipping all these planning and design steps. Instead, you arrive on the morning of the festival without the preparation and without any certainty that you have the right amount of materials. What if the target board you prepped wasn't measured properly and was too big to fit within the booth? What if it did not stand properly because its base was too narrow? So, what if this simple math was skipped and builders made mistakes when constructing a house or a bridge? It's easy to see how quickly math becomes essential in successful building.

Exploring how to use math in the field, in real situations, can foster a stronger connection with the concepts and build excitement for using that knowledge in daily life. This resource goes into several topics. The foundations of arithmetic teach how to make calculations using addition, subtraction, multiplication, and division. Algebra combines these calculations into engaging equations, allowing builders to find unknown measurements on the job site and within the plan. Geometry and trigonometry focus on how to think in terms of shapes, the building blocks of construction. Finally, physics explores what people's creations need to contend with in the real world, such as how a bridge holds the weight of the crossing cars.

USING ARITHMETIC IN CONSTRUCTION

Numbers are everywhere in construction. Even the very basic concept of counting is seen as one of the most fundamental aspects of the job. In fact, every worker will always have a tape measure close at hand. A tape measure is basically a number line used for measurement and can be used to find the width of a window, for instance, or how many feet along a wall a hole will need to be cut. Count along the tape measure to determine length and combine these lengths using arithmetic to construct all manner of projects.

UNITS OF MEASUREMENT

People use different units to express measurements in construction. They depend on scale, or the size of one unit compared to another, and the system of measurement varies by geographic region. Measurements would typically be in the United States customary units (USCS or USC) in the United States, while other places use the metric system. Converting between units is an important skill to have and is vital to reading architectural drawings, planning the amount of materials needed, and proper placement of the structure.

In the USCS, measurements are made in feet and inches and in pounds and ounces. There are 12 inches to every foot, and 16 ounces (oz) to every pound. To convert from feet to inches multiply by 12, and convert from pounds to ounces by multiplying by 16.

The metric system works in meters, centimeters, and millimeters, and in kilograms and grams. To convert meters to centimeters,

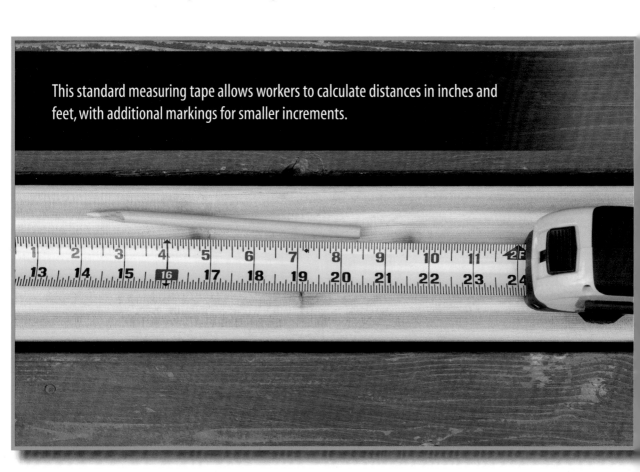

This standard measuring tape allows workers to calculate distances in inches and feet, with additional markings for smaller increments.

WHEN UNITS DON'T CONVERT

Working with the proper system of measurement is essential to completing the job correctly, and being able to convert between systems is vital to making sure that happens. It's common to find some aspects of the work, such as measuring lengths of wood, require USCS measurements, while other tasks require some type of metric unit. In the end, all aspects need to coalesce.

When this relationship is neglected, there can be catastrophic consequences. In late 1998, NASA completed construction of its Mars Climate Orbiter, and the orbiter was launched into a nine-month journey to Mars. Upon reaching Mars in late 1999, the probe miscalculated its propulsion, causing it to fly too close into the atmosphere and burn up. The $125 million loss was due to a lack of conversion between the metric system, which teams at NASA typically used, and USCS measurements used by an external group.

multiply by 100. To convert centimeters to millimeters multiply by 10. There are 1,000 grams per kilogram, so multiply kilograms by 1,000 to convert kilograms to grams.

It is possible to convert between the two systems with an understanding of their relationship. One foot is equal to 0.3048 meters (m). To convert in the opposite direction (meters to feet), multiply by 3.28084.

PUTTING IT TOGETHER

When building new structures or adding onto existing ones, arithmetic is used to add up the lengths of walls and areas of rooms, subtract the size of openings required for doorways, and work with ratios through multiplication and division. For instance, when designing and building the scenery for a stage show you would use the length and width of the stage to find its dimensions. Builders should separately calculate smaller areas off to the side of the stage. Adding the sizes of all regions together would provide a total width or length for the stage and backstage regions.

This approach could also be used to determine the area of the stage in square feet that would be covered by the set design. Determine area by multiplying length by width. For instance, a wall that measures 6 feet tall by 15 feet wide would have an area of 90 square feet. Division breaks apart length or areas into smaller sections. When working on a mural, 30 ft² of wall might need the total volume of one can of paint; of course, the mural will be in more than one color. To cover 90 ft², dividing 90 (the total area) by 30 (the area one can will cover) demonstrates that the project requires the total volume of three cans of paint.

Most work within construction cannot rely on whole numbers alone. Understanding how to work with fractions quickly comes in handy regardless of the size of the job. Converting whole numbers to fractions occurs when converting unit scales or size. For instance, a standard ruler is 12 inches (1 foot) long. Because there are 12 inches per foot, it is useful to describe the same ruler as 12/12 feet.

A great example from everyday life is a typical doorway. The standard door height is 80 inches, which can be described as the

TRY IT YOURSELF

You and a friend are constructing a tree house. Your task is to determine what length to cut a sheet of wood for a wall. You know that the wall will be 8 feet long and 6 feet high, and you want to leave room for two windows evenly spaced across the wall.

1a. If each window is 1'9" wide and will be the same height as the wall, how long does each length of board need to be?

1b. If the windows will be 3 feet tall and will be placed 2 feet above the floor level, what dimensions do the panels above and below the windows have to be?

Construction projects like this tree house can be a great example of math in action during the planning and building process. Note the various angles and shapes that the builder had to create for the project.

11

improper fraction 80/12 feet. Reducing by dividing 12 inches into 80 inches yields 6 feet with a remainder of 8/12 feet. Anyone standing at 6'8" or taller will want to duck their head when walking through a door.

Converting to inches is a technique that can more easily allow adding and multiplying values without fractional representation, and the result can be reduced to a fraction after calculating it. However, with some practice it can be much faster to make calculations directly using the fractions.

Fractions appear regularly when working in construction. For example, the standard 2 inches by 4 inches beam that holds up most walls is actually 1 1/2 inches by 3 1/2 inches after it has been planed to provide a smooth working finish. The typical wall outlet is 2 3/4 inches wide by 4 1/2 inches tall. When building models, they are designed and built at a fraction of their real-world counterpart. It's quickly apparent that many aspects of building rely on fractions to properly measure, calculate, and complete the job.

CHAPTER 2

Using Algebraic Thinking in Construction

Picture the process of building a snow fort. If it needs to fit just one person, it doesn't have to be very big. Once you start adding more people, the size of the fort will need to increase. Additionally, perhaps the height of the walls needs to be adjusted to fit the height of the taller kids. Should it be built with fewer but larger blocks of snow, or would it be better to use many smaller blocks? In the end it may even be a combination of the two, depending on who is building and carrying each block.

As the construction projects become more complex, so does the math they rely on. As more options need to be considered, more variables enter the equation, leading to a wide range of outcomes. Builders need to decide on the best option available that meets their needs. That's where algebra comes in.

BUILDING WITH EQUATIONS

Algebra uses parentheses to group portions of an equation and to identify what calculations should be done first. Consider the snow fort example from page 13. The fort features a wall that is currently six blocks of snow wide but needs to be made two blocks wider. If the wall is also four blocks tall one might write the equation as 6 + 2 • 4. Without parentheses, the order of operations for the equation can be confusing, but the acronym that describes the order, called PEMDAS (parentheses, exponents, multiplication, division, addition, subtraction), always applies. In PEMDAS, brackets ("[" and "]") are used as parentheses. Solving this equation would mean applying the multiplication first, resulting in 6 + 8, or 14 blocks of

When a structure relies on building materials like blocks of snow, a builder should calculate and collect the number of blocks required before putting them together, as this builder seems to have done.

TRY IT YOURSELF

You are building a sandbox and need to determine the length for each beam to make up the sides. Starting with three beams of 6 feet each, you've decided to use two of the beams for the length of the sandbox. The third beam has been split along one end, making 2 feet unusable. Cutting the usable portion of the third beam in half, you nail all four edges together.

2a. What is the total length of wood you used to build the sandbox?

snow. Forming 14 blocks of snow would not create enough blocks to build the fort's wall.

As the PEMDAS ordering shows, grouping the calculations that need to be solved first in parentheses results in the equation being written as $(6 + 2) \cdot 4$. Now the full width can be calculated as eight blocks, and then multiplied by the height of four blocks. To build the wall, create 32 blocks of snow.

VARIABLES: WORKING WITH THE UNKNOWN

When working in construction it is common to end up with only part of an answer. For instance, the architect notes that a wall should be built so that its length is four times the measurement of its height, and only the length of 28 feet is known. To solve an equation involving unknown values, algebra provides the concept of variables. A variable is simply a symbol, typically a letter, that represents some value.

Although the framer does not know the height of the wall, she does know the length. She also knows that four heights are equal to one length. In this case, the equation could be written as $4h = 28$, with h representing the unknown height. To solve for h, the framer can isolate h by doing the inverse operation of multiplication. To do this, she will divide both sides of the equation by four. Doing so reveals that $h = 7$. She will need to cut the beams to accommodate a wall that is 7 feet tall and 28 feet long.

When working with variable equations, applying the same action to both sides of the equal sign can be thought of as applying equally. The equation remains true. To illustrate, consider the equation $3 = 3$. Subtracting 1 from either side would yield $3 - 1 = 3 - 1$, or simply $2 = 2$. The values on either side of the equals sign remain balanced.

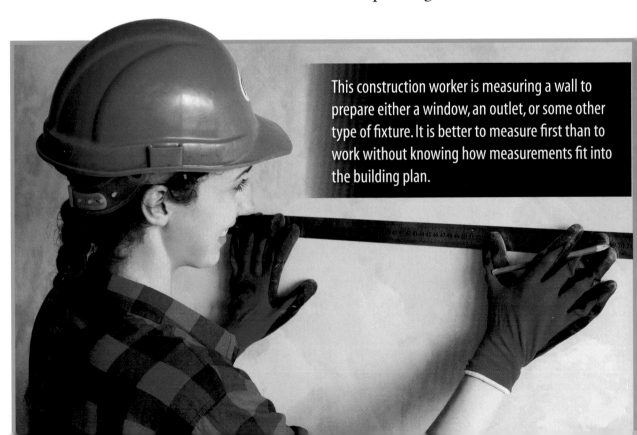

This construction worker is measuring a wall to prepare either a window, an outlet, or some other type of fixture. It is better to measure first than to work without knowing how measurements fit into the building plan.

CAREERS IN CONSTRUCTION

Construction is a broad industry, and the skill sets found there are often used in related fields as well. The following are some of the exciting careers that rely on math.

Carpenters and woodworkers cut and assemble beams to frame houses and movie sets and build furniture. They can also be responsible for intricate carvings and elaborate decorative elements. Similarly, masons work in stone and concrete to build using bricks, to sculpt statues, and to create the foundations that hold the weight of a structure. Math helps to determine which materials to use and how to combine them to support weight.

Architects are responsible for the design and layout of projects. They rely on survey data and an understanding of a building's planned usage to determine its ideal placement. Architects use math to fit the building in the available space and stay within budget.

Specialized roles rely on math to accomplish specific aspects of construction. For instance, plumbers run a specific size of pipes to transport water with the correct amount of pressure. They also ensure that drainage and waste flow safely to the sewer. Energy specialists determine the best way to heat and cool a building, and they are responsible for minimizing losing this energy by using insulation. Even more specialized roles might focus entirely on creating energy using solar power or combining skill sets to make heat using water.

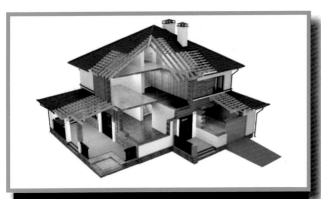

Computer visualizations such as this can be useful during planning. They allow builders to create an easily changeable model that is cheap to create and that accurately depicts the physical reality of a construction design.

But when you're solving for a variable, it's not so easy to be confident that the operation you apply is correct.

One example in which variable usage is essential is when adjusting the scale, or relative size, of a structure. When architects are designing buildings they use a number of tools to define and communicate what the final structure will look like. Paper diagrams or computer models are used to show how rooms connect and what the exterior might look like. Similar to building a model airplane, architects can use physical models to display how a finished building would look while keeping it small. To build such a model, and maintain the proper dimensions, apply a scale.

Using the same scale across the entire building ensures that the relative sizes remain intact. For instance, a warehouse that is planned to be 30 feet tall, 120 feet long, and 60 feet wide could be scaled by using a variable called s. The model's dimensions would now be $30s$, $120s$, and $60s$, and the architect can use whatever scale fits the needs. The only requirement is that the same scale s is used in all instances. If the model needs to be 1 foot long the scale could be calculated using its length: $(120 \text{ ft}) \cdot s = 1$ ft. Solving the equation by dividing both sides by 120, the scale s comes out to be 1/120. That scale applied to all sides of the model results in a model that is 1/4 foot (3 inches) tall, 1 feet (12 inches) long, and 1/2 feet (6 inches) wide.

USING GEOMETRY IN CONSTRUCTION

Working in construction means working with space. Building up, digging down, paving across—these all deal with dimensions such as height, depth, and length. Through the combination of these dimensions, builders create shape: rectangular walls, with circular windows, under a triangular roof. The area of mathematics concerning shapes is known as geometry.

A NEW DIMENSION

A coordinate plane is a space that is used to plot points across an area. The coordinate plane is an extension of the number line into a second dimension and can represent position more so than a one-dimensional value. Once connected, the points create shapes, similar to connect-the-dots. In construction, the coordinate plane helps to determine distances and angles between the points. This process can even work backward, starting with a shape and then identifying points along it.

Points within the coordinate plane are plotted along two axes. One axis runs left to right and represents the x value of a point. A second axis runs up and down and represents a point's y value. The two axes meet at what is known as the origin. Values to the right of the origin represent a positive x value, while those to the left represent negative values. Similarly, values above the origin indicate a positive y value, and those below indicate a negative y value. Each point is represented by a pairing of these values to indicate its position, such as (x, y).

Wireframes and blueprints can be used to communicate floor plans, using a two-dimensional coordinate plane to define the size and scale of a building.

In the construction field, plans are often created using graph paper to make use of a coordinate plane. Using this technique, architects and builders can easily notate the size of rooms, how steep a set of stairs should be, or the angle of the roofline. By identifying what points represent sinks or electrical outlets, plumbers and electricians can calculate the length of pipes and wiring to use. For instance, suppose wiring needs to be run from a circuit box along one wall to an outlet on a neighboring wall.

BUILDING CODES

Each region includes a set of laws and guidelines that specify what materials to use or not to use when building and how to use them. These building codes frequently define a range of regulations including where exits must be placed, a safe distance for placing electrical outlets, and the specifics of how a wall should be built. All stages of construction require observation of these rules, starting with the architectural plans all the way down to the paint applied to the walls once the building is done.

For instance, one such set of rules states that electrical outlets in certain rooms must be no more than 6 feet from one another along a wall. This creates challenges in finding optimal wiring solutions—the types of challenges that can be overcome when planning using a coordinate plane.

Assuming the circuit box is at the origin, at $(0, 0)$, an outlet at position $(4, 6)$ would mean that the wiring needs to run 4 feet along one wall. From where the two walls meet another 6 feet of wire would have to run along the second wall. Altogether, the project requires 10 feet of wire.

Coordinate planes can also be used to find the perimeter of a shape, the sum of its sides. When dealing with four-sided shapes, such as a room, placing walls along each axis can simplify the process of finding the length of each side. This step can be useful when planning how much material to use when building a fence or how many streamers are needed to cover each wall when decorating for an event.

SHAPES AS BUILDING BLOCKS

Designing a building or mapping one that already exists can best be done by finding the shapes it is made of. For instance, a house might appear as a rectangle topped with a triangle, perhaps with a second smaller rectangle attached to the side as the garage. Calculating the dimensions of a building could be a daunting task without the ability to approach the problem one step at a time using these shapes.

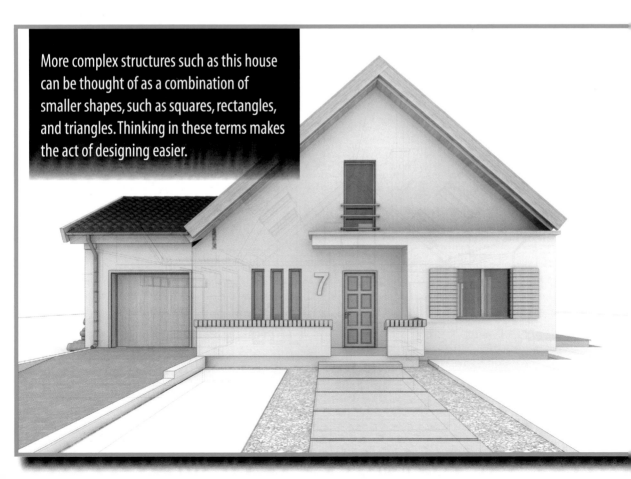

More complex structures such as this house can be thought of as a combination of smaller shapes, such as squares, rectangles, and triangles. Thinking in these terms makes the act of designing easier.

7

Determining area, the space contained within a shape, is a process that people can simplify by dividing up or combining complex shapes into simpler ones. One finds the area of a square or rectangle by multiplying the length by the width. For instance, to find the area contained within a school gym that is 30 feet wide and 60 feet long you would multiply 30 • 60. The result is stated in squared units, in this case 1,800 feet^2. If the gym floor were covered in a

TRY IT YOURSELF

While working on a team to prep the stage for the school play, the set manager asked you to build a ramp to move the scenery. The plan you've received includes coordinates for the stage of (-8, 4) and (4, 4). The ramp should attach from the closest end of the stage to a point at (8, 6). The set manager informed you that the units are measured in feet.

3a. Draw the stage and ramp on the coordinate plane. Then use the drawing to determine the length and height of the ramp.

Note that calculating the length of the ramp itself requires an operation called the Pythagorean theorem. The Pythagorean theorem is $a^2 + b^2 = c^2$, where a and b each represent one of the two shorter sides of a right angle triangle, and c represents the longest side. In this question, you would substitute a and b with 4 and 2. Four squared (4^2), an operation described as 4 times itself, is 16, and 2^2 is 4. It follows that $20 = c^2$, so to isolate c, apply the inverse operation of squaring a number—this is the square root. Thus, $\sqrt{20}$ (also written as $20^{1/2}$) = c.

grid of 1 foot² tiles–tiles that are both 1 foot wide and 1 foot long–there would be 1,800 tiles total.

If a floor plan records the area of a room in two dimensions, incorporating the room's height introduces the third dimension. Space within three dimensions is recorded as volume, typically as units cubed (u^3). If a library plans to cover a wall in bookcases, finding the volume provides the librarian with the space available for new books. In this case, the wall is 12 feet long and 7 feet high. The bookcase being installed would be 1.5 feet deep. When the construction is complete the library will have 12 ft • 7 ft • 1.5 ft, or 126 feet³ of new space to store books, minus shelf space. By approaching construction projects as a series of shapes it is possible to find the size of each section and then combine the totals to calculate the overall area or volume.

This roofless 3D simulation makes it easier to calculate the volume of the space because the height of the room is just as easy to estimate as the length and width.

CHAPTER 4

USING TRIGONOMETRY IN CONSTRUCTION

Trigonometry is a specialized area of geometry focusing on the properties of triangles. Triangles play an important role in construction projects. Triangles are visible in roofs, the supporting structure within the roof, and in ramps or staircases. What's more, triangles are used in construction in ways that aren't immediately recognizable. The grade or angle of a pipe that allows water to flow down and out, and even the invisible angle created when someone looks up at a building are also examples of triangles at work in construction.

RIGHT TRIANGLES

Right triangles contain a right angle. Angles are used to describe the space between two lines that meet. An angle is typically denoted in degrees (°), with 360° representing a full circle. Standing in place and spinning all the way around, returning to your starting position, is a movement of 360°. Since a right angle is a 90° angle, the measure of four right angles total 360°. The coordinate plane has four right angles sitting next to each other around the origin point of the plane.

Squares and rectangles are four-sided shapes with four right angles. Each corner of these shapes is 90°. A right triangle has this same 90° angle, plus two others that add up to 90°. If a square or rectangle were cut in half from two opposite corners, the result would be two identical right triangles. Using this knowledge, it is easy to calculate the area or volume of a right triangle by first calculating for a rectangle using the lengths adjacent to the right angle. Then, divide by 2 to find the associated triangle's area or volume.

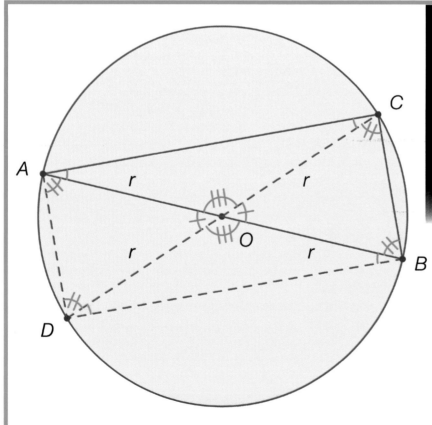

Right triangles can be found within many shapes. Two parallel lines through a circle can connect at the points to form a rectangle diagonally divided into right triangles. One of those triangles is defined by points A, B, and C.

BUILDING WITH MATH THROUGH THE YEARS

Using math in construction is far from a new development. In fact, some of the most well-known structures illustrate mathematical concepts and how they apply outside of a text book. The Great Pyramid of Giza, built more than 4,500 years ago, is the largest of the three pyramids at Giza and is the only one of the Seven Wonders of the Ancient World to exist intact today. Some aspects of its construction used mathematical concepts such as relationships in right triangles that, two thousand years later, became known as the Pythagorean theorem, as well as a strong understanding of the mathematical constant pi (π). In fact, new developments in mathematics have been closely tied to their use in architecture and construction throughout history.

Alongside an existing staircase a developer is installing a cement ramp for accessibility. To determine the amount of cement that will fill the space the ramp requires, the mason must know the ramp's volume. The mason uses the length, width, and height of the box containing the ramp. In this case the box is 10 feet by 4 feet by 3 feet, for a total volume of 120 ft^3. Dividing this in half shows that the mason needs enough concrete to fill a volume of 60 ft^3.

Similarly, adding a roof to a tree house might require a sheet of wood to cover the end of the triangular peak. By finding the width and height of the roof's end, it is possible to determine how much wood to cover it with. In this case, the tree house roof is 4 feet wide and 1.5 feet tall. Multiplying to find the containing rectangle's area, 4 • 1.5, gives an area of 6 feet². The triangular cover needed for the end of the roofline will require half of that, or 3 feet² of wood.

PLOTTING TRIANGLES

The coordinate plane can help with visualizing triangles and is a great tool for working with right triangles. Triangles consist of three points on the plane, with lines connecting them. To draw the slope of a driveway leading up to a garage a builder might plot the points (-15, -2), (0, -2), and (0, 0). In this example, the driveway is seen from the side, ramping up toward the opening to the garage

The coordinate plane helps to map shapes such as this right triangle to usable values including distance and size, and provides a visual means of communicating these shapes.

TRY IT YOURSELF

You are helping to design a birdhouse, with a slanted roof to keep the rain off. The coordinates for the birdhouse are (0, 8), (0, 0), (4, 0), and (4, 8). The coordinates for the roof are (-2, 8), (4, 8), and (4, 10). All values are in inches.

4a. Using a set of coordinates, draw the side view of the birdhouse on the coordinate plane.

4b. Next, determine the total volume of the birdhouse, assuming it is 6 inches wide.

at the origin, $(0, 0)$.

When working with right triangles in plans, builders often use the coordinate plane to highlight the rectangle or box that contains the triangle. This method can help communicate the length and width of the triangle and provide a better understanding of its position and scale within the building overall. For example, laying out a model railroad track can lead to some complex plans. Plotting bridges and hills can require sections of track at an angle to raise the train. These measurements are essential because an incorrectly shaped ramp would lead to the tracks not lining up and would leave the train unable to proceed. To help communicate the size of each section a designer sketches in the width and height of the box containing the right triangle to clearly mark its dimensions. Relying on these details can make a big difference when the time comes to turn the plan into a reality.

CHAPTER 5

Using Mathematical Physics in Construction

Physics is an area of math and science dealing with motion and energy. Nearly every construction project works with, or against, physics. As you add to a tower of blocks they eventually topple over due to gravity. When you fold some paper airplanes you find some fly better than others. Gravity and aerodynamics—how air flows around an object—are aspects of physics. By considering the laws of physics, builders can choose the best material for a job, ensure a building withstands the strong winds it might face, and efficiently insulate against extreme temperatures.

BUILDING WITH PHYSICS

While it may not seem that a stationary building has much to do with physics on the surface, the reality is quite the opposite. A fundamental set of tenets of physics is Newton's laws of motion.

Developed in the late seventeenth century, Isaac Newton applied these three laws to explain a wide range of things, from everyday occurrences to phenomena as grand as how the planets move within our solar system. In essence, Newton's laws can be summarized as:

1. If an object is in motion it tends to keep moving along the same direction and at the same speed, while an object that is not in motion tends to remain at rest. The object only changes its motion or rest with additional force. A nail waiting to be driven into a board remains still until you hit it with a hammer.

2. Applying force to an object will accelerate that object variably depending on its mass. Think about using a heavier hammer to drive that nail. You will need to apply more force to lift and swing it due to the added mass.

3. For every force applied to an object, there is an opposite and equal force returned. When you hit the nail with the hammer you will feel the force applied to the hammer and on to your hand and arm.

In the late 1600s Isaac Newton developed a mathematical theory that explains a variety of physical traits found within the world, including motion and gravity.

In the world of construction these forces of motion are occurring all the time, both while building a structure, as workers apply force with a hammer or backhoe, and afterward, as tenants park their cars in a garage or walk up the stairs. Choosing building materials and using them in a specific way rely heavily on a builder's understanding of physics. One example that you have likely observed at building sites is the truss.

TRUSSES TAKE A LOAD OFF

A truss is a common solution within construction. Its main purpose is to transfer a weight load to other portions of the structure built to bear that weight. By relying on some core physics concepts, a truss is able to manage a large transfer of weight while remaining relatively light itself, so as not to add to that weight. In essence, a truss takes advantage of the rigidity of a triangle and magnifies that support by using a number of connected triangles. Trusses are commonly used in roof frames and bridges, and you have probably seen this telltale web of triangles in action at construction sites or driving across a bridge.

A truss relies on the physics of tension and compression. If you think about walking across a board stretched between two rocks, you might picture the board dipping downward a bit as you reach the center point. When this situation happens you are experiencing tension and compression together—the top of the beam is being compressed inward as it bends, while the bottom of the board is experiencing tension or a pulling outward toward its ends. A truss attempts to distribute the tension and compression caused by the weight it supports across its triangles such that any one side of a

PHYSICS IN ACTION

In 1940, when construction of the Tacoma Narrows Bridge finished, it was opened to the public as the third largest suspension bridge in the world. A common method of building long bridges, a suspension system uses large towers to support the weight of the load. That weight is suspended from the towers using cables that transfer the compression forces to the tower.

Only four short months after its completion, the Tacoma Narrows Bridge collapsed because of an effect caused by the wind known as aeroelastic fluttering. The collapse spurred study into the physics behind the disaster to avoid similar situations in the future.

The Tacoma Narrows Bridge illustrates the construction method of suspending a bridge's weight from support towers, and how this approach interacts with other physical forces.

triangle is either under compression or tension. This distribution allows the weight's load to be transferred to the edges of the truss, for instance to the exterior walls of a house or the endpoints of a bridge on either side of a river. The triangles making up the truss work together so that every part ends up helping with the load.

It is possible to calculate the forces of each length within a truss and determine which are under compression and which are under tension. At its heart, the math is looking at each individual joint within the truss, made up of two and sometimes more lengths creating an angle, and applying some equation to determine the exact forces based on the weight being carried, before moving onto the next joint.

TRY IT YOURSELF

The bridge on page 35 uses a truss system to allow automobiles to cross a river, with supports anchored to the ground at either side of the river. In this case, the truss is built above the platform of the bridge, with the weight hanging from the truss. The trusses allow the bridge to be both strong and light. They also require fewer materials to construct, saving time and money.

5a. Evaluate the truss bridge on page 35. Does it make good use of triangular components?

5b. As a car moves across the bridge, which sections are under compression, and which are under tension?

It is still possible to get a good understanding of how a truss is working without the use of complex equations by applying some mathematical thinking and physics observations. If you study a truss, or even a drawing of one, you can mentally place a weight along its top. Even better, you can build a truss system using Popsicle sticks or similar building materials. With observation you can make a good guess at how that weight might be transferred along the structure. Truss lengths directly below the weight are likely to be in compression, pushed in or downward by the weight. Neighboring lengths are likely to be in tension, compensating for those in compression by expanding outward. This relationship allows a truss system to maintain heavy loads efficiently across a number of applications.

A truss bridge distributes weight and downward-pushing forces to the supports at its ends. It does this by relying on the strength inherent in triangles.

IN CLOSING

With math playing such a vital role in the day-to-day work of nearly all aspects of construction, it's easy to see how rewarding it can be to plan and execute effectively using these skills. From the basic understanding of numbers and their relation to one another, to how to manipulate these numbers using addition and multiplication, to the more complex concepts of geometry and physics math makes up the building blocks of construction. Whether the project is a small assignment for a class, or an extravagant high rise, math will always play an important part.

ANSWERS

Answer 1a. First, determine the overall length of wood to use by subtracting the width of each window from the total 8 feet (96 inches). Converting all units to inches can reduce the need for complex fractions. You are left with 4'6" of wall space to fill. You will need three sections of wood: one for each end and one to sit between the windows. You know that the windows are evenly spaced, which also means that each of the three sections of wood should be an equal length. Dividing 4'6", or 54 inches by 3 shows that each section of wood should be 1'6" (18 inches) long. Each section should be 6 feet (72 in) high, so the total area, calculated as 6 ft • 1.5 ft (72 in • 18 in), is three boards of 9 feet^2 (1,296 inches^2).

Answer 1b. You must find the heights of the wood panels to answer this question. If the windows are 2 feet (24 inches) above the floor, then the panels below the windows will measure 3 ft • 2 ft (36 in • 24 in).

The measurement of the height of the panels above the windows is derived from adding the height of the window, 3 feet (36 inches), to the distance from the floor, 2 feet (24 inches), and subtracting that from the total height, 6 feet (72 inches), as thus: 6 - (3 + 2) = 6 - 5. Those panels will measure 1 foot (12 inches) at the height and 3 feet (36 inches) at the base.

Answer 2a. Count each length used in the construction. A full 6-foot beam is used for each length of the sandbox, but only a portion of the third beam was used for its width. The width of the sandbox is half the beam's length, *after* removing 2 feet, written as (6 - 2) / 2. Filling in the equation above and adding to the lengths yields the lengths (6 • 2) + the widths ([(6 - 2) / 2] • 2).

Solve within the parentheses first to (12) + ([4 / 2] • 2), and then to 12 + (2 • 2). By reducing once more and solving for 12 + 4, you determine that the sandbox uses a total of 16 feet of beams.

Answer 3a. On the plane, the stage appears as a line running from left to right. The edge of the stage at (4, 4) is closest to the top of the ramp, with a line running to (8, 6) representing the ramp. The ramp between the two points runs across a distance of 4 feet, from 4 to 8 along the x axis. The ramp ascends 2 feet, from 4 to 6 along the y axis.

Answer 4a. Start by adding the four points for the house onto the coordinate plane, then connect them to create a rectangle. Next, add the three points for the roof and connect them, creating a triangle that sits on top of the house and hangs off to the left, which will cover the opening.

Answer 4b. First find the volume for the rectangular portion of the house by multiplying its length, width, and height: 4 in • 6 in • 8 in. The main portion of the birdhouse is 192 in^3. Now for the roof portion follow the same steps as if working with a rectangle to calculate 6 in • 6 in • 2 in. Now take this value, 72 in^3, and divide by 2 to find half its value, or 36 in^3. Finally, add the two volumes together to find the total. 192 in^3 + 36 in^3 = 228 in^3.

Answer 5a. The bridge uses triangular structures to maintain a balance of force, distributing the car's weight to the supports at either end. The bridge does make good use of triangular components.

Answer 5b. As the car moves across the bridge its weight pulls down on the beams overhead, applying tension. To compensate, the surrounding beams react with compression as their ends are pushed against one another.

GLOSSARY

ACCELERATION The rate of change in speed over time.

ANGLE The space created between two lines that meet, typically labeled in degrees.

AXIS A line that defines direction and space within a coordinate plane.

COMPRESSION A physical force that increases the density of an object, typically by pressing on it.

COORDINATE PLANE A two-dimensional area defined with two axes, typically notated as x and y.

FORCE Any type of physical strength applied to an object.

FRACTION A number or ratio notated as a/b.

IMPROPER FRACTION A fraction that includes a larger number over a smaller number.

MASS The quantity of matter within a given object.

METRIC SYSTEM The system of measurement that relies on decimal measurements and is typically used outside of the United States.

PERIMETER The sum of the lengths of an object's sides.

PRESSURE A physical force pressing on an object.

PYTHAGOREAN THEOREM A mathematical equation that defines relationships between the edge lengths of any given right triangle.

RIGIDITY The amount of flexibility.

SCALE The relative size of one object or measurement to another.

SPEED A measurement of movement.

TENSION A physical force that stretches an object.

TRUSS A structural component that takes advantage of triangles to maintain strength.

UNITED STATES CUSTOMARY UNITS (USCS, USC) The system of measurement typically used within the United States.

VARIABLE An unknown or changing value used within an equation, often represented by a letter or symbol.

WHOLE NUMBER A number zero or higher; not a fraction.

FOR MORE INFORMATION

American Mathematical Society
201 Charles Street
Providence, RI 02904-2294
(800) 321-4267
Website: http://www.ams.org
The American Mathematical Society supports research, schol-
arship, and education in math and offers publications,
meetings, advocacy, and other programs for the national
and international community.

Association of Mathematics Teacher Educators
Meredith College
3800 Hillsborough Street
Raleigh, NC 27607
(919) 760-8240
Website: https://amte.net
This association conducts research and offers resources and
networking opportunities to improve math education for
teachers and students.

Canadian Mathematical Society
209 - 1725 St. Laurent Boulevard
Ottawa, ON K1G 3V4
Canada
(613) 733-2662
Website: https://cms.math.ca
This society publishes journals, books, and other materials and

offers prizes, scholarships, competitions, and outreach that help students to engage with math.

Mathematical Association of America
1529 18th Street NW
Washington DC 20036-1358
(800) 331-1622
Website: http://www.maa.org
This nationwide membership association hosts lectures
      and other events and publishes communications and
      resources that are meant to support high school, college,
      and university teachers.

National Council of Teachers of Mathematics
1906 Association Drive
Reston, VA 20191-1502
(800) 235-7566
Website: http://www.nctm.org
This council facilitates math education by making sure that
      students can access high-quality learning.

WEBSITES

Because of the changing nature of internet links, Rosen Publishing has developed an online list of websites related to the subject of this book. This site is updated regularly. Please use this link to access this list:

http://www.rosenlinks.com/MYWAU/construction

For Further Reading

Cheng, Eugenia. *How to Bake Pi: An Edible Exploration of the Mathematics of Mathematics*. Philadelphia, PA: Basic Books, 2015.

Cominskey, Michael. *The Number System and Common and Decimal Fractions*. New York, NY: Britannica Educational Publishing, 2015.

Dragotta, Griffith. *Howtoons: Make Anything*. Berkeley, CA: Image Comics, Inc., 2014.

Gladle, Garrett. *Arithmetic: The Foundation of Mathematics*. New York, NY: Britannica Educational Publishing, 2015.

Harrison, Micah. *Perimeters of Ancient Buildings*. New York, NY: Rosen Publishing, 2015.

Marshall, Jason. *The Math Dude's Quick and Dirty Guide to Algebra*. New York, NY: St. Martin's Press, 2011.

McKellar, Danica. *Girls Get Curves: Geometry Takes Shape*. New York, NY: Penguin Group, 2013.

Miller, John, and Chris Scott. *Unofficial Minecraft Lab for Kids: Family-Friendly Projects for Exploring and Teaching Math, Science, History, and Culture Through Creative Building*. Beverly, MA: Quarto Publishing Group, 2016.

Stankowski, James. *Geometry and Trigonometry*. New York, NY: Britannica Educational Publishing, 2015.

Tobin, Jason. *Algebra*. New York, NY: Britannica Educational Publishing, 2015.

BIBLIOGRAPHY

AGC. "Two-Thirds of Contractors Have a Hard Time Finding Qualified Craft Workers to Hire Amid Growing Construction Demand, National Survey Finds." August 31, 2016. https://www.agc.org/news/2016/08/31/two -thirds-contractors-have-hard-time-finding-qualified -craft-workers-hire-amid.

Barnow, Benjamin. *Basic Roof Framing*. Blue Ridge Summit, PA: Tab Books, 1986.

Brain, Marshall. *The Engineering Book: From the Catapult to the Curiosity Rover, 250 Milestones in the History of Engineering*. New York, NY: Sterling Publishing, 2015.

Capachi, Nick. *Excavation & Grading Handbook*. Carlsbad, CA: Craftsman Book Company, 1987.

Ching, Francis D. K. *Building Construction Illustrated, Second Edition*. New York, NY: John Wiley & Sons, 1991.

Emmitt, Stephen, and Christopher A. Gorse. *Barry's Introduction to Construction of Buildings, Third Edition*. Chichester, UK: Wiley Blackwell, 2014.

Freiberger, Marianne. "Perfect Buildings: The Maths of Modern Architecture." *Plus*, March 1, 2007. https://plus.maths.org /content/perfect-buildings-maths-modern-architecture.

Hill, John. "On Architectural Models." World-Architects, November 2014. http://www.world-architects.com/architektur -news/insight/On_Architectural_Models_2247.

Lloyd, Robin. "Metric Mishap Caused Loss of NASA Orbiter." CNN, September 30, 1999. http://edition.cnn.com/TECH /space/9909/30/mars.metric.02/.

Magwood, Chris. *Making Better Buildings: A Comparative Guide to Sustainable Construction for Homeowners and Contractors*. Gabriola Island, Canada: New Society Publishers, 2014.

Mets, Matt. "Ask MAKE: How Do Trusses Work?" Make, June 10, 2010. http://makezine.com/2010/06/10/ask-make-how-do -trusses-work/.

NMSI. "The STEM Crisis." Retrieved August 22, 2016. https:// www.nms.org/AboutNMSI/TheSTEMCrisis.aspx.

Physics 4 Kids. "Newton's Laws of Motion." Retrieved September 13, 2016. http://www.physics4kids.com/files /motion_laws.html.

Scheckel, Paul. *The Homeowner's Energy Handbook*. North Adams, MA: Storey Publishing, 2013.

Wing, Charlie. *How Your House Works: A Visual Guide to Understanding and Maintaining Your Home*. Hoboken, NJ: John Wiley & Sons, 2012.

INDEX

ABOUT THE AUTHOR

Colin Wilkinson is a seventeen-year veteran of the video game industry, where he creates a blend of educational and entertainment titles for young people. As a designer and engineer, he relies on math every day to build exciting new experiences. He lives on a small dairy farm with his wife and two children in a 220-year-old house, where he can find an endless supply of construction projects.

PHOTO CREDITS: